A Conversation with Dr. Michael Quinn: LDS Church Wealth, Succession Crisis, Translation, and Women

(Note this conversation was recorded on November 3, 2017 in Salt Lake City, Utah. I will use GT for Gospel Tangents to indicate when I am talking to Michael. The interview has been lightly edited to remove verbal miscues.)

Introduction

GT: 00:00:01   Welcome to Gospel Tangents, the best source for Mormon History, science and theology, I'm Rick Bennett. I'm really excited to have Dr. Michael Quinn on the podcast. So as many of you know, he's recently written a book, *Wealth and Corporate Power*. We're going to talk about that quite a bit in this podcast and I think we'll give you some eye-opening revelations. We'll also talk about the Succession Crisis, women and priesthood, James Strang, and even Mark Hofmann. So it's going to be a very fun conversation. I hope you check it out.

Contents

Tags: Michael Quinn, Rick Bennett, Gospel Tangents, Deseret Hemp Company, medical marijuana, Wealth & Corporate Power, LDS Tithing, LDS Finances, LDS Investments, Tithing, How does LDS Church spend money, LDS Church expenses, paid ministry, City Creek Mall, God and Mammon, LDS Church spending, money-making operation, Mark Hofmann, LDS Succession Crisis, Book of Mormon translation, James Strang, Women & Priesthood, Ordain Women, Joseph Smith, LDS Succession Crisis, Joseph Smith III, Sidney Rigdon, Brigham Young, Kate Kelly

Michael Quinn Discusses Deseret Hemp Company

Introduction

I'm really excited to have Michael Quinn on the show. In this first episode, we will get more acquainted with him. We will also talk about the Deseret Hemp Company. Yes, I said Hemp! On the ballot this fall is a proposal to legalize medical marijuana here in Utah. Michael Quinn will talk about a church-owned company that grew hemp right here in Utah! Will they get back in the business? Check out our conversation!

The Interview

GT: 00:00:33 Welcome to *Gospel Tangents* podcast. I'm really excited. I've got a real rare treat: Mike Quinn, historian Mike Quinn here in Salt Lake City. So, could you introduce yourself to the audience? Not everybody knows about Mormon history and might not know who you are. Can you give us a little bit about your background?

Michael: 00:00:52 I was born in California and while I was there, we were always told it was the mission field. I became interested in Mormon history as a hobby when I was 16. And then, when I was in the military and after I graduated from BYU in English literature, I had time to reconsider what I wanted to do as a graduate student while I was in the army for three years and I decided to switch to history because my hobby had become too consuming. So, when I came out of the military, I went to the University of Utah to get a master's degree in history. And then I went from there to Yale. But before that I served as a research and writing assistant to Leonard Arrington while he was the Church Historian. After I got my Ph.D. in history from Yale, three months later, I was hired by the BYU campus to join it's a Department of History and I remained there for 12 years and then have been freelance historian or the term is independent scholar in the field, aside from occasional appointments. I had a two-year appointment at the University of Southern California. And then I had a one-year appointment at Yale University and that was my last academic appointment more than a dozen years ago.

GT: 00:02:24   Oh wow, that's cool. So, for those who aren't familiar with your background, I know in the 1980s you wrote a chapter, I believe it was in Maxine Hanks' book,[1] is that right?

Michael: 00:02:39   Yes, it was actually 1992 that it came out. It was called "Mormon Women Have Had the Priesthood Since 1843." And that caused a certain amount of controversy.

GT: 00:02:53   Yeah. Could you, could you tell us a little bit more about that?

Michael: 00:02:56   Maxine was excommunicated. I was excommunicated, and she was specifically told that she was excommunicated because of her book and I was told--I was given a list of three

---

[1] The book is called *Women & Authority*, and can be purchased at https://amzn.to/2M9XuaN

items showing my apostasy, a list provided by the stake president and the first item on the list was that essay.

GT: 00:03:20   Okay. So you're one of the, I guess infamous September Six,[2] right?

Michael: 00:03:26   That's correct.

GT: 00:03:29   So, the one thing that I think would strike most people is a little bit odd, I know I listened to your Radio West interview[3] earlier this week and you mentioned that you're still a believing Mormon. So, some people might think, well, if you're excommunicated, why would you still believe in a church that would excommunicate you?

Michael: 00:03:44   Well, I'm a seventh generation Mormon. Nothing can take that away from me, but even, you know, there are many--well my children are eighth generation Mormons and they talk about Mormons in the third person. They couldn't care less about the church. So, the fact that I'm an ancestral Mormon doesn't determine my faith. My faith is very basic. But it's basic in a way that I think many current members of the church might not understand. In many ways, I'm a 19th-century Mormon believer. I believe in Joseph Smith meeting with angels and translating the Book of Mormon by the gift and power of God, which at that time was a seer stone. And I believe that the leaders of the church from Joseph Smith to the

---

[2] For a brief discussion, see https://mormonheretic.org/2011/05/09/book-review-latter-day-dissent/
[3] See http://radiowest.kuer.org/term/michael-quinn

current president of the church have the calling of divine prophets, seers, and revelators who have the right to receive God's revelations.

Michael: <u>00:04:47</u> But they don't always do so. And sometimes they are too passive in my view, and don't seek those revelations in a direct way. But in my view, they have the right and the obligation to receive those revelations. I don't agree with all the policies of the church and some of them I strongly disagree with and to that extent, although I did not seek excommunication, excommunication freed me from having to defend policies I thoroughly disagree with and that continues until today. So I maintain my faith in a private way. I am in some ways, like a Latter-day Saint, medieval mystic. I have had this feeling even since childhood that it's just you and me, Lord against the world and a God. And my relationship with him was always preeminent. But the reason I always loved going to sacrament meeting on it and as I grew up Sunday school was that the communion was served each at each of those opening services.

Michael: <u>00:06:00</u> And that was always very important to me. And that's one of the things that I miss deeply, as well as the temple. I used to be a temple worker in a variety of ways. I was a temple worker when I was a missionary. I was a temple worker while I was at BYU, a scheduled worker, and so the loss of taking the sacrament every Sunday at least once, and participating weekly as I used to in the temple ceremonies, that has been a deep loss. It's one that I miss all the time. But because I'm kind of this mystic, I'm okay and I don't worry about my relationship with God, but I'm no longer a member of the Church of record, but I'm still—no one can prevent me from believing what I believe.

GT: 00:06:56   So, you still call yourself a Mormon I guess?

Michael: 00:07:00   I do, but not a Latter-day Saint in the sense that I'm not a part of the LDS church. So, if people are attuned enough with the preferred language to ask if I'm LDS, I'll say I'm not a member, but I am a Mormon believer.

GT: 00:07:13   Ok. Have you ever considered the Community of Christ?

Michael: 00:07:16   I've gone to a lot of churches and communions and I love the people in the Community of Christ as I love people in Jewish synagogue. I used to attend Jewish synagogue every Friday and then go to LDS services as well. I love the communion of faith and heritage that is a part of synagogue, or the Jews say temple, going to temple. But, I've never been comfortable in any other fellowship and I really don't need organized religion, for me to maintain my relationship with God. And so, I've never really seriously considered joining any other fellowship, although I've been invited to.

GT: 00:08:06   Well, that's interesting. I'll just a little confession. I actually, when I was on my mission, I went to South Carolina. Me and my companion attended Jewish synagogue for about a month. It was pretty fun on Friday night, so I got to meet the rabbi. He was very nice fellow.

Michael: <u>00:08:20</u>   Well, they're very welcoming people. Unless you try to go to Hasidic or Orthodox, then you're one of the goyim. But it was very fun for me. Initially I started out as a teenager attending reformed synagogue, which was the only one in the town or the city I grew up in, but then when I was attending every week in the military, it was a conservative synagogue, but they welcomed me and they gave me a very, very nice silk yarmulke to attend the services in and always invited me to their Bar Mitzvahs, which you needed to attend by invitation. And they would invite me to those. And they were really, they were sweet people and I really value the fellowship of Jewish people I've known over the years. But I've also enjoyed the fellowship of Muslims and Catholics and of atheists and so I have a broad ranging acceptance of a variety of religious, professions, and religious ideologies. I have a very broad sense of who God loves and who he doesn't. And in my view, he dislikes no one. He loves us all. He weeps for many of us much of the time and for some of us all of the time. But, having felt that way, I feel that I have an obligation as a sinner to embrace all other sinners, even the ones who turn my blood cold. And so even if I don't physically embrace them, I do emotionally.

GT: <u>00:10:07</u>   Interesting. So, tell us why you're here in Salt Lake this week.

Michael: <u>00:10:11</u>   I've been scheduled by *Signature Books* to do a series of book talks and interviews like this, about my most recent book, which is called *Mormon Hierarchy: Wealth and Corporate Power.*[4]

GT: 00:10:26   Well, I'm excited to talk to you about that. So
                                actually, the interesting thing about that book is a
                                narrative isn't that long. It's just three chapters. I
                                was like, oh, I can, I can pound through that
                                pretty quickly. I didn't read all of the tables
                                though. How many pages are the tables?

Michael: 00:10:41   The tables? I'm not sure. There are 17 tables and
                                most of them take at least half the page. One of
                                them or more, is a two-page spread. So, on
                                average I'd say they can maybe take around 15
                                pages of that 150 or so.

GT: 00:11:03   Yeah, there's only 150 pages of kind of narrative.
                                And then there's probably 300 of just appendices
                                and tables and things like that. So the one thing I
                                was leafing through and I thought that one of the
                                businesses had a very unusual name, the Deseret
                                Hemp Company. And I thought, well that's
                                interesting. So, can you talk a little bit? Do you
                                know very much about that?

Michael: 00:11:32   Well, hemp was a textile and people grew hemp
                                the way they grew (I'm trying to think of some
                                other textiles) flax or other things that could be
                                used to make clothing. And Joseph Smith, by
                                some of his neighbors was described as a guy who
                                wore a hemp trousers, which were made from
                                the plant, which was grown in the south
                                generally. And then its final products were
                                shipped north to manufacturing centers in
                                Massachusetts. But in Utah there was this idea
                                that was economically wise, but it didn't always

---

[4] Can be purchased at https://amzn.to/2LMr5aK

work out in practice of Utah's residents being self-sufficient. And so, in order to set up the self-sufficiency, Brigham Young as church president, and for a period of time as governor established a lot of missions with an economic basis. So, there was a flax mission, there was a cotton mission, which of course also caused the textile industry in Utah to grow. And then there was a hemp-growing process, although it wasn't exactly a hemp mission, but there were general authorities who were involved in the growing of hemp and, and its use in manufacturing shirts and trousers. So that was similar. It was a similar kind of enterprise to the cotton mission that Brigham Young had established in southern Utah, but that lasted longer, and it was more successful. And as far as I know, I have no evidence of anyone smoking any of the hemp.

GT:	00:13:20	{chuckling} That's what I was worried about.

Michael:	00:13:22	No.

GT:	00:13:23	Ok. Do you know when that ended, that hemp?

Michael:	00:13:25	It was a kind of short lived. I'm not sure why it didn't last as long. The wool mission was an animal byproduct. But that lasted a long time. And so, did the cotton mission, which was a plant product both used for textiles, and manufacturing clothing. I'm not sure why, I don't know the details of the hemp manufacturing. Perhaps it's more difficult to do, and it may or may have needed more chemicals which they would have had to import and that might have diminished the appeal of trying to manufacture locally grown hemp into locally manufactured clothing.

GT: 00:14:06   Did they actually try to grow that here in Utah?

Michael: 00:14:08   Oh yeah. Yeah.

GT: 00:14:10   Ok. Did it last into the 20th century?

Michael: 00:14:12   No, no, no. In fact, none of these did. The cotton and the wool church-owned businesses basically ended around the turn of the century in the early 1900s. And so, the clothing manufacturing that did continue for a period of time with General Authority and Church investment, didn't depend on church grown products, whether it was wool or whether it was cotton. By the time of the early 20th century, there was a secularization that was beginning. And so, the church products were often shipped to distant locations that had little or no Mormon population and they were importing products, raw materials as well. So, the effort at being totally self-sufficient really ended around the 1880s, not long after the death of Brigham Young.

GT: 00:15:17   Okay. Okay. So, 1880s, that's good to know.

Are LDS Church Revenues really $50 Billion/Year?

Introduction

In our next conversation with Dr. Michael Quinn, we'll talk about how much money the LDS Church earns per year. Would you believe it is as high as $50 Billion? Dr. Quinn breaks down how much comes from tithing and for-profit businesses, and also states how many church members pay tithing. Are LDS General Authorities expected to pay tithing? Check out our conversation.

GT:	00:15:20	So with your book, I think, at least for me kind of a big headline, that I think most people have noticed is how much tithing does the church make and what's your best estimate on that?
Michael:	00:15:35	Well, the tithing has to be understood as a revelation that was dictated by Joseph Smith in a form of "Thus Sayeth the Lord," and what he said the Lord was saying to him in 1838. But from 1838 to 1900 for most of the 19th century, the definitions of tithing changed. And the adherence to this commandment changed too. And initially it was very, very onerous for a convert to obey the law of tithing as it was defined in the late 1830s to early 1840s. Because what it required was a convert to donate to the church ten percent of everything he owned, or she owned, and then 10 percent of your annual increase after that. And despite that, thousands of people joined the church. But then under Brigham Young, this was liberalized, although that's a bad word for many

Mormons today. It describes what he did and that is, he made it less onerous to live the law of tithing.

Michael: 00:16:51   And it was only 10 percent after the initial years of the settlement in Utah, when these poor people that already paid 10 percent of everything they owned, were expected to pay 10 percent upon arrival in the Salt Lake Valley of what they owned at that point, which usually wasn't much. And those onerous requirements were finally in the 1850s ended. And by the late 1850s, all that was required was to give 10 percent of your annual increase, which is the term of the revelation, or interest, which was also a term that was used. But most people from that time to the present, would think of it as your annual salary or your annual profit, the annual money that you made as income. And so, that was the requirement from the late 1850s onward, but few members of the church lived it and it wasn't until 1900 when a president of the church was faced with more than $2,000,000 debts that the church needed to pay and had tremendous servicing of the debt, which meant that the church had to pay interest on these debts.

Michael: 00:18:15   And also I had to borrow to even pay the interest. Lorenzo Snow in 1900 made a dramatic push, you could call it, or dramatic appeal to the faith of the Latter-day Saints to begin to pay more regularly on a regular basis, their tithing so that it could be a source of income for the church that they could depend on and to more completely fulfill the 10 percent requirement. And from 1900 onward, this became a more emphatic requirement. But even then, by the 1920s, the Presiding Bishop of the Church announced in General Conference that only 25 percent of the church membership paid a full tithe. And the rest paid either what was called a part-tithe or no tithing at all. So as a membership of the church at no time, I think it's fair to say, has the membership of the church totally adhered, even the devout membership of the church have they totally adhered to the requirement of paying 10 percent of their annual income.

GT: 00:19:33   So, it sounds like it was quite some initiation dues between 1830 and 1850 in order to even join the church.

Michael: 00:19:40   Right, and yet thousands did. And then it was liberalized to 10 percent only on an annual basis. And eventually you have the annual interview with a bishop. And I don't know exactly when that came in, but I think it was in the 19th century, not the 20th, when that became a pattern, whether it was required by church headquarters or not.

GT: 00:20:05   Tithing settlement is what you're talking about.

Michael: 00:20:07   Yes, that's now what it's called. But the idea that it was decided on the local level, whether you were a part-tithe payer, or a full tithe-payer was in place in the 19th century. And so that has continued to the present. The General Authorities do not make that decision even for themselves. The General Authorities meet with their bishops in their local wards of congregations and like every other rank and file member of the church are asked, "Do you pay it a full tithing?"

Michael: 00:20:41   And they either can ask an answer, yes or no. And then the follow-up question is, "Do you pay a part-tithing," yes or no? And then the follow-up question is, "Are you exempt," Yes, or no? And people who are exempt are often--it depends on sometimes church policies which are varied. Missionaries have been exempted from paying tithing. People who are on church welfare have been defined as being on tithing, or pardon me being exempt from tithing. But those have typically been the only exemptions allowed. Somebody who is a church General Authority, for example, who has no other source of income, but what the church gives him, it's still expected to pay 10 percent of that back to the church. Otherwise, and I've seen the PBO[5] reports. He is defined as a part or no tithe payer.

GT: 00:20:41   Do they take away his temple recommend?

Michael: 00:21:45   Right, it could happen and it wouldn't be the first time that a general authority has been threatened with being dropped from office for one reason or another.

Michael: 00:21:57   But, in the tithing reports that I had access to from the 1890s to 1928, typically a general authority who said he was a part-tithe payer was only in that status for a year or two. And then he became a full-time payer. Whether there was

---

[5] I believe PBO stands for Presiding Bishop's Office. The Presiding Bishop is in charge of church financial affairs for the entire church.

pressure applied, I don't know. But, sometimes it did last more than one year.

GT: 00:21:57 Oh Really?

Michael: 00:22:26 Yeah. But, typically the general authorities were recorded as full-tithe payers.

GT: 00:22:31 Yes, I would expect they should be.

Michael: 00:22:33 Anyway. The tithing has never been 100 percent in payment. And in fact, in the 1990s, a *Deseret Book* publication said no more than 50 percent in the '90s, which would be a dramatic improvement over the 1920s. But, it's always been a part, even of devout members of the church who have paid a full tithing.

GT: 00:22:57 I would be surprised that it was as high as 50 percent because we keep hearing activity rates are about 50 percent and I wouldn't expect everybody who came to be a full tithe payer.

Michael: 00:23:06 Right. And this was only an estimate by a non-General Authority, but it was one that the *Deseret Book* allowed to be published under its authority. And so, its editors really allowed that to be stated whether it was accurate or not, I don't know. But, the lowest level that I have reported by a member of the Presiding Bishop was 25 percent and that could be the area that it's hovering around maybe 25 to 40 percent pay full tithing. But it depends, because I've heard praise given during the Cold War. For example, I heard praise given by General Authorities for the members of the church in East

Germany, which was a communist, very repressive regime that they paid 80; 80 percent of its membership paid a full tithing of what little they had. And this was remarkable. And I saw no reports of the international church.

Michael: 00:24:14   And so I'm only going by what was said over the pulpit by general authorities in praising the devotion of members of the church in East Germany during those years, from the 1950s to the 1980s. But, that was something that was frequently I heard praised over the pulpit, not only at General Conference, but sometimes by visiting General Authorities who in stakes I attended would make a comment about that tremendous devotion. So, it varies and I'm sure it varies internationally and people who are very poor give the widow's mite and this would be true of the poor in many developing countries who barely have enough money to feed themselves and their children. And yet many of them are not exempted from tithing despite that poverty and they do their best and then some succeed to pay 10 percent and still keep their kids from starving. So, I don't think we should be flippant about the fact that many people don't pay tithing.

Michael: 00:25:20   Many people who don't pay a full tithing are just barely getting by. And sometimes it's a matter of do I pay full tithing, or do I feed my children or clothe them or give them shoes? And that's not just a problem in America. There's poverty in north of Mexico as well. But in developing countries it's a severe problem. And so, I think that those who do pay full tithing in the United

States should not feel self-righteous about it because in the Philippines, for example, government statistics indicate that the average Filipino family can only provide one meal a day for every member of the family. And so those who do pay or struggle to pay a full tithing are really paying similar to the widow's mite which Jesus praised.

GT: 00:26:20   So, what about church businesses? If I remember right in the book you said you believe that the church makes about $33,000,000,000, per year. Do you have any idea how much church businesses bring in?

Michael: 00:26:37   Well, I had the exact figures of church tithing paid annually, in the period down to 1928. Then again, in the period of the 1940s and in the 1950s up to 1962 and I could give you down to the penny how much church headquarters received in tithing from members of the church. After that point, I don't have those kinds of figures and so I made a projection in the book based on the growth rate of tithing and it was growing at an annual rate during the 1950s and I felt that that was a conservative way of projecting because in the 1950s the church was sending missionaries to war torn Europe which was still rebuilding from World War II, to war torn Asia, which was still rebuilding from its devastation in Japan and the Philippines and elsewhere from World War II.

Michael: 00:27:39   And then sending missionaries and building churches, not only in those countries but also in Latin America where in the 1950s one percent of the population own 90 or more percent of the country's wealth. And that was true in every Latin American country. And so, during that time period, the growth of the church still in that decade of the 1950s averaged 12.9 percent annual increase of tithing. So, I felt that that applied in the future would be a conservative measure of the future growth of the Church's tithing. So, I applied that on an annual basis from 1960 to 2010 and I had an ability to check the first years to see how accurate my projection was because I had the tithing figures for 1961 and 1962. And what I found was that my projections in that table were significantly below the actual tithing that the church received in 1961 and 1962.

Michael: 00:28:52   And so I felt confident that I have chosen a measure that was conservative. Using that straight-line projection, the amount that comes up for tithing alone in 2010 is $33 billion (with a b) dollars. Now on top of that is what I call commercial: income from for profit businesses, which are by their definition are for profit; profit from sales of generally nonprofit businesses like welfare farms to the general public, which in those cases are made like Deseret Industries sells to the public and even though they sell at a very moderate rate, that is taxable income by state and national standards. And then there is the portfolio of the church which is stocks and bonds and how much they make or don't make on that. And so, I have several measures jumping decades of what that was in 1900 and 1902, those sources of income, which I generally call commercial income, accounted for almost 18 percent of the Church's total revenue those two years.

Michael: 00:30:25   And those were not years when the church's businesses were doing wonderfully. Some were, many were not. Then again, in 1928, about 29 to 30 percent of the church's total revenues came from businesses and from investments. Then in the 1960s and 1970s, N. Eldon Tanner, who was a member of the First Presidency was given responsibility for the financial life of the church, he told two different reporters for two different financial magazines, that in the late 1960s as well as in the late 1970s, the church was receiving about 50 percent of its income from tithing and the rest came from investments and for-profit businesses. And so, I estimate that by that it's conservative or reasonable to assume that 40 to 45 percent was coming from those sources.

Michael: 00:31:37   And in the later interview he gave in the late 1970s to a Canadian financial and business outlet or magazine, he said that the investments of the church, he limited to blue chip stocks and bonds, which meant the highest pay, the most secure, the least risk involved, in those highest levels of investment. So, you can take your pick. The estimates from Church headquarters have been too low. They've been lower than any of those verified estimates of particularly church headquarters from the 1950s to the 1990s have said, five to 10 percent. That doesn't match any of the figures that I have from 1900s to the 1920s to the 1960s to 1970s. So, whether you take the low-ball amount that I know is accurate in 1900s of 17 percent extra beyond tithing or N. Eldon Tanner's estimate in the 1960s or '70s of 40 to 45 percent, we're talking billions of dollars on top of the Church's, $33 billion tithing that I estimate, as commercial income. So, I think you could say $10 to $15,000,000,000 a year as of 2010. We're coming from the various kinds of commercial investment businesses that are for profit by definition, nonprofit businesses that sell some of their products to the public and therefore are taxed on those sales. And then the very large portfolio of the church and to indicate how large it is, the investment houses, which again is a generic term I use, are scattered and they know about each of their own portfolios that they handle for the church, but they don't know about the other investment houses and what they handle and how much profit or loss they have in a particular day or particular month or particular year. But the central investment house from the 1990s on to the present as far as I know, is called Ensign Peak Advisors and the president of Ensign Peak Advisors spoke with *Deseret News* in 2003.

Michael: 00:34:20   And he said that each day his company, handled billions of dollars and that's only one of the investment houses of the church. So, I think that my estimate of tens of billions is probably close to the mark of commercial income from all sources, not just the portfolio, but also for-profit businesses and nonprofits like welfare farms that also sell some of their produce to the public and are taxed on that.

GT: <u>00:34:57</u>   So let me make sure I'm clear on that. So, you're
                                      saying roughly $33 billion a year plus another $10
                                      to $15 billion on business income.

Michael: <u>00:35:07</u>   So, I would say as of 2010, $40-$50,000,000,000
                                      in total revenues from all sources.

Would LDS Church Income Ever Support a Paid Ministry?

Introduction

As we saw in our last episode, the church makes perhaps $40-50 billion per year between tithing and church businesses. Dr. Michael Quinn has noted that church members no long pay building fund, ward budget, and many other expenses due to this large income. Is there enough income to support a paid clergy? Is there a scriptural prohibition against paid ministers? How much money does the LDS Church spend in foreign countries? Check out our conversation....

Michael: 00:35:16   However, having said that, a huge amount of the annual revenues of the church goes into paying for the services of the church to the rank and file. As many people outside the church know, and all Mormons know, the church has primarily an unpaid ministry, volunteer ministry of people, men and women who work, and provide for their own wellbeing outside any income that they might receive from the church.

Michael: 00:35:53   They are, essentially what you know outside the church is called a lay ministry. Only a very few, I'd say less than five percent, ninety five percent being unpaid, less than five percent receive what's called a living allowance. And these are the General Authorities who serve for 24-7 for life in most cases, or a few of them serve for a five-year to six-year basis for 24-7. And then also temporary appointments, like the General Authorities who serve only five or six years, mission presidents serve usually a period of two to three years. Temple president serve usually a period of five to six years and they are also 24-7 during that period of service. And they receive living allowances. But what's called the church administrators, those are paid jobs. That's a part of what outsiders or people like me would call the bureaucracy of the church.

Michael: 00:37:02   The church preferred term is church administrators, but they receive salaries and those salaries are subject to taxation. Those salaries include benefits and retirement benefits and health and hospitalization benefits because these are paid employees of the church, but they're not paid to minister. They are paid to handle administrative things such as handling the Church's fleet or being in charge of the architectural designs of the church. And they receive their paychecks from church headquarters, but they're doing "secular" kinds of jobs. They're typists. They're accountants, they're programmers, they're truck drivers. There are a variety of capacities that receive their pay from the church and they are expected to pay 10 percent of that to the church if they're an employee of the church. And if they're reported to headquarters by their local bishops as not paying a 10 percent tithing, eventually the church bishop or stake president will be told by Church headquarters to inquire why is this church employee not paying 10 percent? And that's true of BYU Faculty. And that was my case when I was on the BYU Faculty for 12 years. I was expected to pay a full 10 percent and actually worked out with all the other things Mormons were required to pay at that time, contributions to the missionary fund, contributions to church welfare, the fast offering fund and budgets for maintenance of local buildings and all of that. That added up to anywhere from 12 to 15 percent total of one's income. And because of the financial growth of the church, not just tithing, but dramatically because of its commercial income. By the 21st century, the church had ended all of those additional contributions except tithing so that all of those are now paid by central headquarters for members of the church in Canada and United States as well as for members of the church in other countries, including the developing world.

GT: 00:39:29   Yeah. So, I remember as a kid growing up, my dad did pay budget. And I also remember one of the interesting things was, I lived back in New Hampshire. When I was 10 years old, we moved there. We actually for church, met at high school, Merrimack High School and did that for a couple of years. And then, we built a church in Nashua, New Hampshire. And I remember we had to raise money to build the church. Like that was not tithing and all that. And we had moved from Utah. And I remember, this was kind of funny. My mom knew how to make corn dogs and we made, you know, a few hundred dollars selling corn dogs and everybody in New Hampshire was like, what's a corn dog? They'd never heard of that. And so, it was kind of like an exotic food almost.

GT: 00:40:22   But I can remember we did fun runs and it was all for the building fund. And so, the stake center there in Nashua, New Hampshire, I remember at the time, it was the largest church in New England. It was considered gigantic and you know, it was just regular size stake center. You wouldn't think anything of it here in Utah. And it was nice when, you know, that was probably 1980, I believe when that happened. and it was nice when all of a sudden, the church says, well, we're going to start paying for all the buildings and we didn't have to do these fundraisers and things like that.

Michael: 00:40:56   Members of the church who have either joined the church in the 1990s or became reactivated in the church after years of being away may not recognize this because they've not been required to pay maintenance for their local buildings, which was called ward budget. They have not been required to pay for building the buildings, which was a building fund and that was in operation as long as the building was under construction and sometimes when they had to make a replacement, repairs, or buy a new pipe organ that also had to be a separate budget. Well, when I was moving around as a graduate student, graduate students as well as people in management of businesses frequently move. I knew families, some of whom were students and others of whom were in executive positions in stakes, mentioned to me that they had paid a budget, a requirement for building a new chapel, building fund where they had previously moved. They moved into the stake that we now lived in and they were hit with another building fund from a new church that was being built for their ward. And so, in the space of a year they had paid for two different buildings, one of which they were not even able to use because they'd moved before it was completed. But they've paid into the construction of it and those kinds of things don't exist anymore. And that is because of the financial stability that has come to the church since the 1980s in particular.

GT: 00:42:44   And I think that's great. So, in a sense, we've gotten a break since the 1980s, you know, on just paying tithing. We don't out to pay anything else.

Michael: 00:42:53   And that also applies to supporting missionaries because it used to be that the amount that your families were expected to pay for you and were told that they would need to pay on a monthly basis as a missionary was based on the cost of living where you lived. And so, people who went to developing countries paid very little for the missionaries and people who went to Paris or London or New York City as missionaries had to pay a much higher amount. And in the 1990s that was standardized for all missionaries throughout the world are expected to pay a very reasonable amount. And in developing countries, in many cases that the church pays that for families who are really too poor even to pay that modest--from North American, north of Mexico, point of view, modest amount of monthly support for a missionary even if his requirement or her requirement in New York or Paris or Tokyo might be stratospheric for the living allowance. The family only pays very moderate amount. Well even that moderate amount in the developing world is beyond the ability of parents of these missionaries. And so, in cases, that are known to the local leaders' mission presidents, missionaries who want to serve in their own countries typically serve for 18 months or two years.

Michael: 00:44:29   Most of their living allowance is paid by the church for these missionaries. And so, members of the church in North America, north of Mexico, United States, and Canada have a relatively easy payment requirement or donation requirement. I mean, it's not a requirement in the case that someone's going to come with no neck, men dressed in black at your doorstep and {in a gruff voice} "we know how to deal with you people."

Michael: 00:45:05   But, it's a requirement for the faithful and the faithful feel an obligation when they're asked to do something voluntarily to do it. Well so many of these--which would amount in many cases to about five percent of their income, they no longer have to pay. And now all that's required is tithing, and the fast offerings that were required are in a sense not—there is kind of a tradeoff. You give the value of the money you would've spent on two meals and you give that to the church. And so, it technically is not an additional requirement beyond tithing. And so, you know, I think that this is a wonderful thing that the church is able to do that it was not able to do for more than 150 years of its existence and because of the financial stability and the commercial income of the church, that's no longer an expectation.

GT: 00:46:12   Well, let me ask you another question. You know, one of the things in the LDS Church that we kind of pride ourselves on, and I don't know if we should pride ourselves on it so much, it was the fact that we do have a lay clergy. You know, I'll tell you what. I went to the Community of Christ back in August and Lachlan MacKay, an apostle for the community of Christ gave a Sunday school lesson. It's one of the best Sunday school lessons I've ever had. It was on the Word of Wisdom.[6] At first, I was rolling my eyes. It was fantastic. But my question is, you know, like with the building fund that we don't have to pay anymore because that all rolls into tithing. Could you ever see the church paying clergy, even down to the level of a bishop to do that? If we've got enough income to do that, could you ever see something like that happening?

Michael: 00:46:58   Well, this is one of the ironies. Even though the 19th century church frequently used the insulting phrase "hireling priests" for Catholic and Protestant ministers, the revelations in the Doctrine and Covenants which maintain these "thus sayeth the Lord" documents that Joseph Smith provided during his lifetime. They provide for a paid ministry. They say the laborer is worthy of his hire and that could justify having a thorough paid ministry all the way down to the local level. However, there has always been this discomfort with providing for the living of the leadership of the church, whether it's general

---

[6] See our discussion: https://gospeltangents.com/2018/01/24/surprising-word-wisdom-insights-apostle/

leadership or the local leadership. And so, for a period of time there were no salaries given to the general authorities. They had to live by what they could receive as voluntary offerings, unsought for by the local members or what they were able to earn. Brigham Young, for example, was a painter and a carpenter. He brought in some money that way as an apostle. Other money just given to him as a free donation, freewill offering is the phrase.

Michael: 00:48:21 But because of this really unpredictable amount that they received, some of the general authorities, some of the apostles, we're simply on the edge of poverty and most of their lives. A set salary system was finally established after the deaths of Brigham Young in 1877 in the fall, October actually. And there has been a sort of salary system. Again, the preferred term is living allowance from that time to the present. And initially it was set up on a stratified basis. The president of the church received the most each month, and that would translate to a year, but they had monthly payments. His counselors received the next most, the senior apostles received the next, the junior apostles received the next. The Presiding Bishop received the next. His counselors receive the next. And then the senior members of the Seventy received the next and the junior members of the Seventy received the next.

Michael: 00:49:26 And the lowest always wants the Patriarch to the Church, but that office discontinued in 1979 and no longer is a part of the leadership of the highest leadership of the church. And in the 1960s, the president of the church finally did what other presidents had been moving toward gradually and that was equalizing the living allowance given to all general authorities and that has been in place since 1966 and continues today where the president of the church receives the same living allowance as the most recent appointment as General Authority. Now, some of these men are independently wealthy before they accepted an appointment as a prophet, seer and revelator, or a member of the Seventy. And in such cases, they choose on their own to donate their living allowance or not to accept that at all, but those who are not wealthy, they need that living allowance.

Michael: 00:50:36   But again, it does not go beyond the general authorities of the church except those temporary full-time positions such as temple president, mission president. And it has not extended down to local stake presidents who have exclusively in their calling a religious obligation to fulfill of what is typically defined in Christianity as ministry. And, I think even despite the growth of the church, I doubt that there will ever be for these local officers over congregations, the kind of living allowance that would allow them to serve full-time. The tradition of the church, and it really is a tradition, it is not required by the revelations that the members of the LDS Church honor as God's word. It's not required that all of the service in the church be on unpaid. But I think the tradition of the church is strong enough, it has gone on for 180 years, to prefer an unpaid ministry. I think that will continue at the congregational level. And so, I don't ever expect to see those local officers, whether in mission fields or in stakes, which is a distinction Mormons recognize outsiders wouldn't. But, I don't think that will ever change.

"The Church Makes No Distinction Between God and Mammon"

Introduction

There are many critics of the LDS Church's wealth. Is the LDS Church guilty of serving God and Mammon? I asked Dr. Michael Quinn that question, and I think you'll be surprised by his answer. We're going to talk about the City Creek Mall. The LDS Church paid $1.5 Billion dollars to make it. Michael Quinn says that this enormous income allows the church to spend enormous sums of money to support LDS Church growth. It's not just in poor countries like South America and Africa. Quinn says that the LDS Church has deficit spending even in rich countries like England. Is it true that the City Creek Mall is subsidizing churches in poor countries? Check out our conversation....

GT: 00:52:18   Ok, interesting. So, I wanted to talk to you a little bit about some of the things that critics complain about with the church, the City Creek Mall, one and a half billion dollars. Now at least until I read your book, I had no idea how much the church made. So that sounds like a lot of money. But when, if they're making $50 billion a year, one and a half billion, it's really not that much money. What would you say to critics of the Church that would complain and say, well, why are we investing into luxury apartments and high end [fashion] Victoria Secret, which isn't even really [modest by LDS standards.] With the modesty rhetoric Victoria Secret wouldn't be a store that we would expect that most--that would uphold chastity standards, let's say. So, what would you say to critics of the City Creek Mall specifically?

Michael: 00:53:13   Well, I'd say that in one sense, from the 1830s to the present, the business of the church has always been business. If members of the church look at revelations in the *Doctrine and Covenants*, they'll see revelations from the early 1830s about establishing a tannery, establishing a lumber facility, establishing merchandising in 1841, a revelation about building a hotel. And so, these are built into the concept of revelation that God does not make a distinction between the temporal and the divine, between the moneymaking and the spiritual, that operating a lumber company or operating a store can be as spiritual as giving aid to the poor in the Mormon concept of reality. This is very different from other religious traditions, but it's a part of the Mormon definition of reality. Brigham Young continued that. He dictated one time, he says, "Some of you members of the church," and this was happening even in the 1860s.

Michael: 00:54:30   He said, "Some of you complain because I haven't issued revelations. I could issue revelations every day." And he announced a word of the Lord revelation to the conference of the church about building railroads. And it was a "Thus Sayeth the Lord" kind of revelation. And, his successor John Taylor issued "Thus Sayeth the Lord" written revelations that have specific texts, although never added to the Doctrine and Covenants in the 1880s about investing in gold mines and silver mines. So, this has been a part of Mormonism from its earliest origins to its pioneer time in Utah to the present. And so, I understand it can disturb people when they hear that a million point five, LDS headquarters has` acknowledged, paying upfront for the construction and furnishing to the degree was necessary of the environment of the City Creek Mall. However, put this into context not only with the income of the church but with these expenditures.

Michael: <u>00:55:49</u>   In 2006, the LDS Church headquarters gave a cash supplement to the church in the United Kingdom of nearly half a billion dollars, $450,000,000 and change. And that was in one year to one of the countries in which the church has had a significant presence since 1837. It is an industrial country. It is not a third world country. Its members are generally thought of as being comfortable. This is not the case in any country. Mormons can be poor even in the United States and there are poor members of the church who live on government welfare and church welfare in the United Kingdom. Well, the tithe payers in the United Kingdom couldn't pay all of their responsibilities, all of the building and the maintenance and the missionary work and everything else, the aid to the really poor that occurs in the United Kingdom. And so in one year the church gave nearly half a billion dollars. I mean, I don't know the total number, but I know it's more than 100 countries throughout the world the church is in.

Michael: <u>00:57:08</u>   In third world countries, and there are at least 50 and there could be far more than that. The church, and I have the reports to demonstrate this, is paying 90 to 95 percent of their expenses are being paid in cash from church headquarters on a year by year basis in the developing country or what in during the Cold War used to be called the third world. The church could not do this if it didn't have billions of dollars, not only of tithing, but of commercial income from for-profit businesses, which the City Creek Mall is intended to be for. It's stock and bond portfolio, which is totally separate from the investments in the City Creek Mall. So, the City Creek Mall wouldn't be possible without all of this investment and profit, nor would the life of the church, even in industrial countries like the United Kingdom, which has averaged between 50 and 60 percent of its expenditures, have to be paid on an annual basis, by Church headquarters and 90 to 95 percent of the developing world.

Michael: <u>00:58:23</u> The church couldn't do that without this gigantic amount of income. And then you compare that to the president of the Church since 2012 when it was raised to $120,000 a year. That's the top salary level or living allowance level of the general authorities. And I didn't think of doing this, but at one of my presentations in recent weeks, somebody in the audience said, "Mike, do you know that the, that the CEOs of charities make substantially more than the president of the church?" And the example of this person gave was the Red Cross. The CEO of the Red Cross makes a million-two or a million-five a year. That's just salary not benefits. And compare that to one-tenth the amount that the president of the church and subordinate general authorities are given as a living allowance. And to me this is faith promoting. The highest amount of the expenditures of the church goes for building the church, for benefiting the rank and file throughout the world.

GT: 00:59:39   Of that $50 million that the church makes, do you have an idea of how much they use to subsidize other countries and missionaries and things like that?

Michael: 00:59:50   Well, with other countries, it's very clear from the Philippines and from Tonga their reports I have on an annual basis and it works out to 90 to 95 percent. So, you think of the church in Latin America and the millions of members total from Mexico to Tierra del Fuego in Latin America, 90 to 95 percent of their expenditures are paid by church headquarters as an added supplement. I don't know this by having read their reports because their reports as required would be in Spanish and I don't know the accounting language in Spanish, but I have these English language reports from the Philippines, which are no better off financially than the members of the church in Latin America on average. Tonga, where the church has 50 percent of its population are on the records of the LDS Church.

Michael: 01:00:46   And the same as in Tonga, close to 90 percent on average of its expenditures are paid by the LDS Church on a regular basis. So, in Latin America, it's millions of members are being subsidized to 90 percent. In Africa, in Ghana, and Nigeria alone, those two countries in sub-Sahara Africa, the church has more than a million members of record and yet those Ghanaians and those Nigerians cannot afford to pay for their chapels. And in many cases, there is an effort to make their chapels convenient for the people who live in villages and so they may not be more than what would be called an arbor or bowery with a shade area and tent poles. But even that construction is, unless they do it themselves from their local produce or the local building materials that they are able to get locally, that has to be paid in money by church headquarters because the members of the church in Ghana and Nigeria and Lagos and all of the other (well Lagos is the capital), but in Togo and many of the other countries of sub-Sahara Africa where the church has total, and not counting the Republic of South Africa, which is a wealthy country on average, the church subsidizes.

Michael: 01:02:23   But even the Republic of South Africa in the one report I have available for the, the Republic of South Africa, they were deficit spending. And by that, I mean they were spending more than their tithing allowed them to spend on. So, they were receiving even in a country which is one of the wealthiest of Sub-Sahara Africa, if not the wealthiest, they were not able to meet all their expenses with their own timing. They also had to receive a tithing supplement or an expense supplement from LDS headquarters. So, you add up all these countries throughout the world that are developing countries, Sub-Sahara Africa, Latin America, Oceana, Asia, including the Philippines,

which I do have their reports, 90 to 95 percent
are being paid by the headquarters of the church.
The church is spending billions of dollars a year in
supplementing the tithing that these relatively
poor members of the church are paying as they
can throughout the world.

GT: 01:03:41   So let me ask this question. I'll phrase it this way.
Would it be accurate to say that the City Creek
Mall, and maybe even Victoria's Secret, is
subsidizing some of these buildings in Nigeria?

Michael: 01:03:57   Without question. I mean, in the book, I lay out
those that I'm aware of through the Internet. And
there is a remarkable openness on the Internet to
the Church's investments in a variety of areas,
whether it's land where the produce is primarily
going for the welfare program. But what they
can't use for the welfare program would spoil if
they didn't sell it to the general public. And that's
for profit. So, there are profits that even Deseret
Ranches of Florida, which is a welfare outfit in its
original definition, it's also for-profit and it's
making millions, maybe billions. I mean I don't
have the financial records, but at least millions in
its annual revenues and all the others, there are
apartment complexes that the church is invested
in, aircraft storage hangers.

Michael: 01:04:59   It's like why would the church do that? Because
there's money to be made. And the Church is in
all of these, and oil and gas, mining, the Church is
in all of these areas, high profit areas where it
determines through its advisors that this is a good
money-making operation. And they have it in

40

Florida and in Missouri that I know of. The church has created entire communities from scratch that cover multiple areas, zip codes, and these are for profit. They sell these homes in some cases for millions of dollars per home, in other cases, $300-$500,000 a home and this is moneymaking. Yes, it costs money to create these homes to build them, but then it's profit once they sell them to those investors, mainly non-Mormons, but partially Mormons who buy these homes and these communities, whether it's near Orlando or near Independence, Missouri or wherever it might be.

Michael: 01:06:10   The church is very shrewd investments and so yes, in merchandising, there is no longer a church owned merchandising store. Zions Cooperative Mercantile Institution for more than 100 years was church owned, ZCMI merchandising operation, and it had branch stores throughout Utah, Idaho, and even some of the adjacent states. Besides those two. those no longer exist and the church instead of rents space to May Company, and to other companies.

GT: 01:06:10   Macy's bought ZCMI, so they probably rent to Macy's.

Michael: 01:06:54   and Macys, and Nordstrom's, and so they are in the position of renting space on a monthly or annual basis for these profit making companies. And so when you buy their products of these companies who were lessees of the church-owned property, whether it's, at City Creek Mall or elsewhere, their profits, whether it's book sales or food or lingerie or washing machines, whatever it may be, those are contributing to the net profits of the church.

Michael: 01:07:32   And down the road in a trickle-down way, those are benefiting the developing world in where people can very often not pay more in their own ability for more than one meal a day for each member of your family.

GT: 01:07:43   Could the church be accused of serving God and Mammon though, with some of these businesses?

Michael: 01:07:48   The accusation is there, but typically it comes from people who don't recognize that the church makes no distinction between God and Mammon. The church is a money-making operation, but it plows the money into the building of the Kingdom of God on earth, which is a Mormon phrase that most members, even disaffected ones, will recognize. A member of the church, whether former member or current member in good faith, may feel uncomfortable with this huge portfolio that involves billions of dollars a day in transactions over the computer with only one of its investment houses.

Michael: 01:08:34   It may be [that] members of the church and devout members and certainly ex-members of the church are uncomfortable, or may be uncomfortable with the commercial real estate that produces and the commercial investments in mines and oil, for a variety of reasons, not the least of which would be fossil fuels. For people who are concerned about that. And the Church has heavily invested in fossil fuels. Nonetheless, it's a part of building the Kingdom of God.

GT: 01:09:09   Should the church be more concerned about global warming?

Michael: 01:09:12   That is a decision. For many, many years the church has refused to invest in, and refuse to accept the stock until it can be turned over as soon as possible of a tobacco company or of a liquor manufacturing company donated by non-members, in many cases, to the church. People may not realize that the church receives significant stock and real estate investments from non-Mormons who admire what the church does. And in talking with one of the managers of the Church's financial investments forty years ago, he told me that as soon as one of these came across his desk as soon as possible, he sold it and used the proceeds to buy stock or bonds that were profitable. But within the parameters the church defined as its own and legitimate.

Michael: 01:10:13   The church can make those decisions whenever it chooses. And it might one day choose to exclude a fossil fuels. But right at present, it's not an obvious violation of revelations of the Lord and if they choose to do so, it will be a management decision of policy. Not necessarily of "Is this a theologically sound thing?"

Michael: 01:10:43   It may be a matter that this is a policy that we would like to discontinue because of these concerns for the environment. That is a decision, because the church has governed by members of

the conservative parties in their various countries
generally, that may be a long time coming. I
regret, even more so than I would regret them
having portfolios with liquor or cigarette stock,
which they don't keep. I regret that there is
investment in fossil fuels, but it's very lucrative as
anyone who's invested in those companies know
or hear their annual reports. Just read the report
of Shell or of Unocal, or of any of the large
companies, Mobil Oil. They have enormous
profits in the billions annually and they're proud
of those. And you know, that's a management
success story. I would like the church to divest for
those, but I'm not offended by the fact that the
church invests in those kinds of companies. It's
just if I had my druthers, I'd rather them think of
those companies in the way they think of tobacco
and alcohol as ultimately doing more danger than
the investment profits are worth.

Quinn on Hofmann

Introduction

Michael Quinn has been a very prominent Mormon historian since at least the 1980s. I asked Michael if he had met Mark Hofmann, the bomber and forger. Michael indicates that he may have inadvertently given Mark some ideas for forgeries! I also asked Michael if he was worried about being targeted by bombs. Check out our conversation!

GT: 01:12:21   Alright. So, one of the questions that I have actually, I have a thousand. I may have to book you again for another interview {chuckles}. I've been talking with a few people about Mark Hofmann. So, I don't know. You probably haven't followed some of my recent interviews: Shannon Flynn,[7] George Throckmorton,[8] who was the man who discovered how Mark was doing his forgeries. Were you involved with Mark Hofmann at all?

Michael: 01:12:55   I met Mark Hofmann typically at meetings where we would cross one another in the hallway. There was sometimes when he was on a panel. I don't think he ever gave a full presentation of his own, but he was on a panel discussion usually talking about some marvelous find of his church history. And I've attended one or two of those that I remember, but usually at the Mormon History Association or at Sunstone Symposium we would

---

[7] Part 1 of our interview with Shannon Flynn is at https://wp.me/p8l6gx-j6

[8] Part 1 of our interview with George Throckmorton is at https://gospeltangents.com/2018/06/26/george-throckmorton-hi-fi-hofmann-forgeries-murders/

kind of pass one another in the hall, say "Hi, how are you?" And he would go off to whatever session he was interested in and I would go off to whatever I was. And not often were they the same? The only other times that I met with him was when I was at the [LDS] Church Archives doing research. Typically, I avoided taking lunch. I would be there from the time the door opened until the time they threw me out.

Michael: <u>01:13:51</u> And I would never take a break for lunch or rarely take a break for lunch, but I would be in there typing my notes on whatever document I was examining and he would come in sometimes alone, sometimes with someone else who is an associate with him in one way or the other, and would come over and interrupt me. And I'm barely civil to people who interrupt me when I'm doing research. And so, I would [say], "Yeah, that's very interesting. Yeah. Let me get back to what I'm doing." And so those were the kinds of conversations I would have with him. There was one time when he brought in the typed text of a document that he said he'd found in some attic and was happened at that time to be a document about the blessing of Joseph Smith, III, and he said, "Well, what do you think of this?"

Michael: <u>01:14:48</u> And it was like, "Wow, I'm interested in this." And I asked him if I could take notes.

Michael: <u>01:14:48</u> "No."

Michael: <u>01:14:48</u> "Can I type my own copy of this?

Michael: <u>01:14:48</u>   "No."

Michael: <u>01:14:57</u>   Even though what he showed me was the typescript and I never did see any of the documents that he was producing in real form. I only saw photographic productions of them usually as published in the *Deseret News* or the *Salt Lake Tribune* or wherever, or sometimes in an article that was published in *BYU Studies* or whatever about them. And so that was the extent of our association. The only other thing that I did is I recommended, because I'd given up trying after years of trying to contact descendants of early Mormons who I knew had diaries and there were two in particular that I recommended to him to follow up on what I knew. And one was William McLellin, whose diaries I had found described in a letter at the New York Public Library.

Michael: <u>01:15:58</u>   And I had tried to follow through his obituary, all the surnames of his descendants, not just McLellin, but daughters who had married, mentioned in his obituary. And then a man named Sylvester Smith who died also in the Midwest. McLellin died in Missouri and was a distant relative, really more of a shirttail relative of the Smith family, not a direct relative of theirs. Sylvester Smith died in Nebraska. And so, his obituary said that he had kept a diary since he was 12 years old and I thought, "Wow, this is something I want." And he died in about 1885 or so 1882. And the obituary listed all of his descendants who were living by name and so I followed not only the descendants named Smith, which was going to be very difficult, but I also followed the children, his daughters who had married with other surnames.

Michael: <u>01:17:10</u> I went that through telephone books and I got every telephone book in the Midwest for both these people, McLellin and the in-laws of Sylvester Smith and I'd given up. I'd written hundreds of letters to these people over a period of years, never gotten back an answer from any of them. And I'd really just written it off as a lost cause. And so I made recommendations for the McLellin descendants and for the Sylvester Smith descendants. So, I gave what I had in terms of the evidence of their keeping diaries during their lives to Mark. And I said, "This is what you do. You contact descendants and you've been very successful," I thought. And so, "Here's what I know about the evidence of their keeping journals." And he said he would, follow up on that, let me know.

Michael: <u>01:18:08</u> And then in the early 1980s, I was hearing that he had found contacts in the McLellin family about McLellin's papers and so I was really upset that he hadn't let me know that he had made this contact. So I wrote him a letter and I said, "I gave this information to you years ago and you promised to keep me in the loop if you were successful. And I've heard through some of your friends," who are mutual friends of mine, 'that you've made the contact with the McLellin family and have his archives so to speak. And I said, "I expect that you should allow me to at least see these and take notes on what I think is interesting." Well, I never heard back from him. And then one day in 1985 in early October after the Sunstone Symposium I was walking into the BYU library and he happened to be walking out and I said, "Did you get my letter?"

Michael: 01:18:08   "Yes."

Michael: 01:19:18   And, I said, "well, you know, I think you owe me the opportunity to examine."

Michael: 01:19:23   And he said, "Well, I'm bound by agreements I've made with the descendants," and he said "I'll have to check with them."

Michael: 01:19:29   And it was very obvious he did not want to talk with me about this and that he was uncomfortable and he kept looking at his watch as I was talking to him. And so that was the extent of the last interaction I had with him. And then a few days, weeks later, boom, boom, boom. And he killed these people in premeditated murders. And everything fell apart from that tIme forward, including his forgeries, his life of forgeries that he'd started when he was quite a young man. But that's the extent of my [interactions], you know, you've got it. Everything that I knew about him and through personal contact, that was the extent of it.

GT: 01:20:13   So were you pretty surprised that he was actually the bomber?

Michael: 01:20:20   Oh Yeah. I just thought this was not the Mark Hofmann I knew, who was just very shy, very retiring person. I mean, I talked about him being uncomfortable and talking and looking at his watch, but the other times he barely got eye contact. I thought he was one of the shyest people I had met in Mormon History Association and typically I learned more about what he was doing from friends of his, like Brent Metcalfe who frequently socialized with him. I never socialized with Mark Hofmann and I don't think--he never invited me to, even though I was interested in things he was interested in and I passed on some of the leads that I had for getting stuff that I thought was in attic somewhere in the Midwest.

Michael: 01:21:10   And it turned out there were. But these people who acknowledged at one point receiving letters for me, you know, it was like, "Who is this guy?" And he's connected with BYU and why should we believe him? And, they were contacted eventually by a reporter from the *Salt Lake Tribune*.

GT: 01:21:28   So he probably got some ideas for his forgeries from you.

Michael: 01:21:32   And he may have from things I published. Yeah, because typically I would talk about things that weren't available that were central, like I published an article about the Council of Fifty minutes and the Council of Fifty's history and I commented about what I thought was in those minutes that I had not seen of the Nauvoo Council of Fifty. And so, I would do this about other documents like I wrote about the blessings that Joseph Smith, III had received from his father and that obviously was something that Mark

Hofmann paid attention to. But in terms of conferring with them and, you know, planning out strategies, the closest I came to it was giving him these two sources about William McLellin and about Sylvester Smith that I thought would lead to him contacting somebody who had something squirreled away in an attic. And that was about the only consulting I ever did with him.

GT: 01:22:40   So you weren't concerned about getting blown up or anything?

Michael: 01:22:44   Well, I got calls on the day that he was blown up with the one that he had in his car. The people at the time thought it had been planted in his car. I was told, "Don't go back to the apartment you're living in," because at that time I was newly divorced and was living in a bachelor apartment and so I had a friend who worked with the state attorney, U.S. attorney was in his office and this long-time friend of mine called and said, "Don't go back home, go and stay with us because no one would think of us," him and his wife. And so, he provided more than a week I think a week or two weeks of residence for me during this period.

Michael: 01:23:36   And then he told me, "When you go back, look under your car for wires," and for years after this, following his advice, anytime I got a package I wasn't expecting, I would take it to the post office and run it through their x-ray machine to see if there were any machines in it. And so yeah, I was paranoid.

GT: <u>01:23:58</u>   Wow. So it was pretty widespread. There were a
                                  lot of people that were scared.

Michael: <u>01:23:59</u>   Yeah.

LDS Succession Crisis

Introduction

Dr. Michael Quinn is one of the foremost experts on the LDS Succession Crisis. He says there were seven legitimate succession claims following the death of Joseph Smith. In a previous interview, John Hamer said Sidney Rigdon was the best option according to canon law. I'll ask Quinn that question, and we'll talk about some of the other candidates. Check out our conversation...

GT: 01:24:04   Now, you mentioned the blessing, the patriarchal blessing for Joseph Smith III. One of my interests has been to talk a little bit about the Succession Crisis. So, as I understand it, if Joseph Smith died, the next person in line would have been Hyrum Smith.

Michael: 01:24:19   He was joint president and everyone understood this and Joseph did not want him to go to the jail with him because Joseph Smith thought that this would be the end of him, being in Carthage Jail.

GT: 01:24:19   The end of Hyrum, or Joseph?

Michael: 01:24:19   The end of him, himself.

GT: 01:24:19   Joseph, ok.

Michael: 01:24:40   But other men went with him, including Hyrum and Hyrum wouldn't leave.

GT: 01:24:47   And so Hyrum wasn't actually arrested. He was just there to support Joseph.

Michael: 01:24:53   He was there and none of the other men who were there with him. The arrest warrant was for Joseph. It wasn't for any of those. And when I say the attenders, or the other occupants of his cell in Carthage Jail, none of them are under indictment and none of them had been arrested.

GT: 01:25:12   So it was only Joseph.

Michael: 01:25:12   Um, hmm.

GT: 01:25:20   So, I know John Hamer has said that with both Joseph and Hyrum dying at the same time, the person most likely to succeed was probably Sidney Rigdon.[9] It wasn't Brigham Young.

Michael: 01:25:28   It could have been a variety. In the article that I published in 1975[10] years before Hofmann came out with any of the wonderful documents {sarcastically} that he came out in Mormon history about, I said that there were seven legitimate ways of succeeding Joseph Smith, that he had made provision for, either within his published revelations or within things that he had done that were well known. And Brigham Young was only one of them. Sidney Rigdon was a surviving counselor, was only one of these methods. And, Brigham Young and the 12 apostles was in many ways a distant possibility by revelation. But in terms of what Joseph Smith did in policy at Nauvoo, with regarding the Quorum of the Twelve, they became a more likely a

---

[9] See our interview at https://gospeltangents.com/2018/01/13/different-succession-claims-mormon-groups/
[10] See https://byustudies.byu.edu/content/mormon-succession-crisis-1844

succession option because of the power that he had given them within Nauvoo itself, which was the headquarters. Typically, by the revelations, the authority of the Twelve ended when there was an organized state with a stake president. They had no authority within a stake. And so, the stake president of the central stake, who at that time was a William Marks had a claim.

Michael: 01:27:01   And so I looked at all of these. So, I would disagree with John Hamer that Sidney Rigdon was the most likely. He was the first publicly proposed alternative to the Quorum of the Twelve and he was voted down by the congregation that met in August of 1844. When their choice was only Sidney Rigdon or the Quorum of the Twelve, they chose the Quorum of the Twelve to continue in the Twelve's position in its place of having all this prior role administratively within Nauvoo, the headquarters of the church. And they rejected Sidney Rigdon. But the fact that he was the first publicly proposed doesn't mean that either one of them was the most likely. That was the choice that the Quorum of the Twelve and Sidney Rigdon had advertised. And this had been advertised before the Twelve was even back in Nauvoo. Most of the apostles, members of the Quorum of the Twelve were in the eastern states, and there were only one or two members in Nauvoo and two of them were wounded in and the attack on Carthage Jail.

Michael: 01:28:30   Willard Richards, the least wounded, got a bullet through his ear lobe. And John Taylor got four bullets in his body. He was riddled with gunshot.

And so he was near death at a certain point, severely wounded by the August meeting, able to limp up onto the stand as one of the Twelve. But you know, during that summer, the one who was being privately promoted the most, particularly by Emma Smith was William Marks.

GT: 01:28:33   Oh Wow.

Michael: 01:29:04   The stake president. And she used the published Doctrine and Covenants as the reason for him being the next president of the church. So, that's why I say that in terms of those at church headquarters, it was either the Twelve or William Marks. Those who were in the know about how little Joseph Smith respected Sidney Rigdon by 1843 and 1844 knew his name wasn't even mentioned in those discussions that were going on that we know about through the diaries of the apostles and through the diaries of Joseph Smith's private secretary.

Michael: 01:29:50   And also through the diary of Joseph's tutor, the tutor that he had hired for his children. He was living in the Mansion House of Joseph was murdered. And his in his diary also shows how William Marks was the one that Emma was talking about and arguing for. So, Sidney Rigdon wasn't even on the screen of most of those who were at the core of leadership and of Joseph Smith's life, including his widow. But Sidney Rigdon came back to Nauvoo before the Quorum of the Twelve. He set up this meeting and this meeting was to choose between what he gave as the choice to the members of the church: "me or the Quorum of the Twelve?" And he thought for sure that the church would choose him over this group, which was scattered around even at the death of Joseph Smith.

GT: 01:29:50   Well didn't William Marks support Sidney Rigdon as well?

Michael: 01:30:54   He did. He did, even though he could have made-- and there was a doctrinal revelatory reason that he could have been far more powerful an advocate of his own claim than the Quorum of the Twelve, who by the revelations had no authority in an organized stake. And he was president of the central stake at Church headquarters, but he never advocated himself. If he had it could have been really rough going for the Quorum of the Twelve because it was easy to dismiss Sidney Rigdon, who was a loose cannon and mentally unbalanced and people had known this for more than a decade.

GT: 01:31:43   So why did Joseph pick Sidney as his Vice presidential candidate?

Michael: 01:31:44   Because he had religious background. He was a minister, well known in the group that later became the Disciples of Christ. And, he was a leader who was a very forceful speaker where Joseph Smith wasn't. He knew the Bible as well as Joseph Smith. Joseph had virtually memorized it. But he was accustomed to speaking, public speaking for years before Joseph and he met one another and that was not the case with Joseph. Joseph was shy and he spoke with a whistle after

1832 because he'd been smashed in the face by a mob that had tarred and feathered him. And so, after 1832 at the time that he established counselors and a First Presidency, he chose Sidney Rigdon as his spokesman because Sidney Rigdon had a presence. He was an orator who could sway crowds and often spoke to crowds for hours at a time. And Joseph Smith, one of the early devout members of the church, talked about a meeting where Joseph spoke. And then Sidney Rigdon spoke, and Hyrum spoke and, and the devout member of the church, who was Jared Carter, in his diary said, "Well, Joseph gave one of his pathetic sermons."

GT: 01:31:44   Oh Really?

Michael: 01:33:21   Yes. And then we heard a wonderful sermon by Sidney. I mean, so he was not a known as the speaker in the 1830s. That changed. And by the 1840, he impressed non-Mormons who heard him speak in Nauvoo. But that was a growth period for him. And in the 1830s he was a very shy person.

GT: 01:33:51   Ok, so you've said Sidney Rigdon, Brigham Young in the Quorum of the Twelve, William Marks. Who are some of the others?

Michael: 01:33:54   The patriarch for the Church who at Joseph Smith's death or soon after was his brother William, who was not ordained patriarch until after Joseph Smith's death and he was ordained by the Quorum of the Twelve and he was himself and a member of the Twelve. But as soon as they gave him the position of presiding patriarch, he began saying, "I'm like Hyrum Smith who was patriarch of the church and I have the right to be the president of the church." I mean the Twelve never regretted anything as much as they regretted letting him become the Patriarch to the Church.

GT: 01:33:54   He didn't last as Patriarch very long, right?

Michael: 01:33:54   No, not very long.

GT: 01:33:54   Was it six months?

Michael: 01:34:42   Yeah. And that's because Brigham Young was as consolidating his support at headquarters and elsewhere, but primarily headquarters. And so that was another option. And a third option was a son, not just a patriarch, but a son, and his son was 11 1/2 when he died and that was Joseph III. And it's very clear to me from the evidence that he expected his son one day to lead the church, but not when he was 12. And so, it was a thing way down the road, decades, because Joseph Smith's own statements and one of his revelations indicated that he expected to live until he was in his eighties. And so, by then, Joseph III would have been in his sixties and that would've been a good time to surrender the reins of the Kingdom of God to a son. So, although Joseph had the plan for his son, undoubtedly to be an apostle, maybe patriarch for the church instead of one of Joseph's Smith's brothers. Joseph Smith did not expect to die at the age he died, 39, until it was too late. And it was too late to designate anyone else. I mean, he was dragged from Nauvoo by officers of the law.

Michael: 01:36:05   And the people he spoke with, he was saying goodbye to. "I'll never see you again," because he knew he was done for. And his only hope was that the Nauvoo Legion would rescue him, and they didn't. And the mob that came initially, he thought it was the Nauvoo Legion, to spring him out of jail. And that wasn't to be.

GT: 01:36:35   I guess Mark Hofmann even invented a letter about that from Jonathan Dunham. Can you talk about that?

Michael: 01:36:40   Well, yeah. Jonathan Dunham allegedly and according to members of the church and these accounts were fairly well known in Utah that members of the Church in Utah said that Joseph had instructed Dunham to bring the Nauvoo Legion to Carthage and rescue him. And the Nauvoo Legion, not too many people realize this, but as an organized military body was second only to the US army in 1844.

Michael: 01:37:19   And, if Dunham had brought it to Carthage Jail, the jailers couldn't turn away a mob of a little over 100, if that much. They certainly couldn't have turned away the 4,000-member Nauvoo Legion that Joseph Smith was the commander of and the second in command in that time period was Dunham. According to informants in Utah and some in Illinois, Joseph had given instructions that "If I'm taken to jail, you are to rescue me." And Dunham declined because Dunham knew it would be a blood bath if he did. Not at Carthage Jail, but the aftermath, because here Joseph Smith was accused of treason for destroying a printing press and a newspaper. What would have been the response of the governor and of all the other county sheriffs, including the one in the county in which Nauvoo was located, if Dunham had brought a private army of Mormons to rescue Joseph Smith from county jail where he'd been sent by legitimate authority and taken away from the rule of law.

Michael: 01:38:45   I don't think there would have been anything that could have stopped a united attack on Nauvoo by people in retaliation for this unlawful springing of Joseph Smith from Carthage Jail. And so, Dunham refused to obey the command. Now, I doubt that the command was written. Because there wasn't a document, Hofmann forged one. But, I think the stories that Dunham turned away from an obligation to save Joseph, were circulated enough that it was something that he understood at least as a verbal order from Joseph Smith.

GT: 01:39:45   Ok, so you think that there really was a verbal order to spring Joseph.

Michael: 01:39:45   Yeah.

GT: 01:39:45   Really? Where do you...?

Michael: 01:39:51   Well, there were a number of people who, in talking about those who were at the jail. I haven't looked at these documents for a long time, but there was a history of the Nauvoo Legion for one that was a manuscript history that I cited. I cited it for another reason, but within that Nauvoo manuscript that was written sometime between 1845 and 1846, Joseph had given the order to Dunham to rescue him. And, this was why Dunham and was rejected. This was later stated by people and published in various accounts of Joseph Smith's death, written by some non-Mormon, some by iffy Mormons, in the 1850s and 1860s as being a rumor that was being circulated. And the death of Dunham was often ascribed to guilt over having disobeyed that order. And that comes also out of this early history of the Nauvoo Legion that was written within Nauvoo. Because of guilt, he asked another member of the Nauvoo Legion who happened to be a member of the Council of Fifty, the theocratic body to kill him, to blood atone him, which was the term that was used.

GT:	01:39:51	To kill Dunham?

Michael:	01:41:35	Dunham, as a recompense for having allowed Joseph Smith to be murdered in Carthage Jail rather than following his duty of rescuing him. And Joseph wouldn't have required that. I think Joseph was a forgiving person. But, those who blamed Dunham for the act felt this sense of good riddance when he went off with a Native American whose identity we know and disappeared in the wilderness. And, everyone said good riddance.

GT: 01:42:16   Wow, that's interesting. Okay. So that was very
                     interesting about Jonathan Dunham. I did not
                     know that.

Joseph and Strang Translation Process

Introduction

We're continuing our discussion of the Succession Crisis. James Strang was a big rival to the Brigham Young movement. He claims to have a letter from Joseph Smith putting him in charge of the LDS Church. Dr. Michael Quinn tells why he believes the letter was a forgery. Strang was known to translate the Voree Plates. How does that compare to Book of Mormon Translation Joseph Smith did? Michael Quinn tells his beliefs about the translation process of the Book of Mormon. Check out our conversation…

GT: 01:42:16   So let's see. I think we've come across five. The other two, I think one was James Strang.

Michael: 01:42:31   James Strang and it wasn't specifically James Strang. It was ordination as a specific successor. Originally the precedent for that was David Whitmer. Joseph Smith had designated him in 1834 to be his successor. And so that was an option as well. And then the Council of Fifty was the seventh.

GT: 01:42:55   Oh, okay. The Council of Fifty. Okay. So, what do you think about Strang's claim?

Michael: 01:42:58   Absolute fraud.

GT: 01:43:00   Really?

Michael: 01:43:02   Oh yes.

GT: 01:43:06   Oh Wow. Why do you say that?

Michael: 01:43:08   The document itself was hand-printed.

GT: 01:43:09   Okay.

Michael: 01:43:10   The signature was hand-printed.

GT: 01:43:12   Really?

Michael: 01:43:15   Joseph never did that. No, it's an absolute fraud.

GT: 01:43:17   Absolute fraud.

Michael: 01:43:18   Yeah.

GT: 01:43:19   I know that some...

Michael: 01:43:20   But he was a charismatic fraud, which is why people followed him because Brigham Young did not come across as charismatic even though he spoke in tongues and sang in tongues. And he announced revelations and he had dreams that he thought were very significant. But he was not perceived as a charismatic person. He came across in a different way, and none of the other potential ones came across as charismatic. Rigdon was a great speaker. He had a silver throat and silver tongue, but he was a loose cannon and mentally unstable and many of the Nauvoo residents knew that. But Strang came along with claims of being the charismatic associate and successor. He never knew Joseph Smith, never had any personal contact with him, despite the claim that he did.

Michael: <u>01:44:28</u>   And he proclaimed himself as a new prophet and people were hungry for that because Joseph Smith had not published a revelation since 1841. and that was published in the church periodical, but none since then. And so even in Nauvoo there are people saying, "What have you done for me lately? Where are these revelations?" And so, there were people who were impatient for the word of God to be delivered, "Thus say it the Lord," even while Joseph Smith was alive, those last two or three years of his life. And the rank and file knew nothing of what he was teaching privately about God's revelations concerning the theocracy and the Council of Fifty, plural marriage, and the endowment. Those were very heavily guarded secrets. And so, the rank and file were the ones most influenced by this claim of [James Strang] to be a new prophet.

Michael: <u>01:45:27</u>   And he began dictating revelations and he began translating ancient records and then he began mimicking Joseph Smith and other ways. I went through his papers that are primarily and not exclusively at Yale. And he had even a private group of initiated people into a secret fellowship, men and women, and he had ordinances connected with that. Eventually he secretly re-instituted polygamy. And because he was this charismatic alternative to Brigham Young, those who had already fallen out with Brigham Young for other reasons like Joseph Smith's brother William, and men like some members of the council of Fifty and others who saw Brigham Young as not the kind of leader that they want it to follow, gravitated to Strang. And Strang left open, kind of tantalizingly, the possibility for a living son to descend and to have prominence if not the successorship.

GT: 01:45:27   One of Strang's sons?

Michael: 01:45:27   Well no, one of Joseph's sons.

GT: 01:45:27   Oh, one of Joseph's sons.

Michael: 01:46:56   And so for this reason, members of Joseph Smith's family, his mother, his sister, and William Smith signed to document endorsing James Strang. Emma didn't sign the document, but nearly everyone else in the Strang families still living did. So, Strang had a lot of pull as a member for a period of time. Strang's followers rivaled those who were following Brigham Young on the trail to Utah and Brigham Young saw him as a real threat because Brigham wasn't, you know, he had dictated this one revelation that became eventually part of the Doctrine and Covenants published in Utah, but most people knew of it only through excerpts published here and there. And Strang was just dictating one revelation after another and translating ancient scriptures that he had dug up.

GT: 01:47:56   Yeah. John Hamer actually gave a presentation at Sunstone just a couple of months ago and said that he looked at the I'm pretty sure it was the Voree Plates, very short thing, but he said you could actually translate it. I'll be publishing it soon. But John actually viewed it and I'd be curious your opinion, he said that he felt like it was a more legitimate translation of these plates, which John's not claiming that they're legitimate, but the translation of them makes more sense than say the Anthon Transcript. John doesn't really believe in a historical Book of Mormon. So, and I don't know how you feel about that. Do you have an opinion on the Book of Mormon?

Michael: 01:48:46   Yes, I believe it is written based on ur-text? I believe it's tribal history. The way the Old Testament was tribal history originally told around campfires and that the Book of Mormon is based on an actual ur-text, written ur-text, Gold plates. I believe those. But I don't think that everything in the published 1830 Book of Mormon derives from that ur-text, derives from that ur-text. That's a German phrase: Ur-text meaning the original text. I don't believe that. I mean, there are things in there you can see as Joseph Smith's understanding of the Bible. You can see things in there that reflect attitudes of the people at the time. You can see things where he's reacting to attitudes of the people of the time. You can find that evidence there and I can't deny it. And so, I don't deny that there are 19th century evidences are in the Book of Mormon, but there are other things, as a faith claim, as well as other evidences in there that I find persuasive as relating to an ur-text, relating to what had been written on gold plates.

Michael: 01:50:05   But Joseph Smith had no ability to translate any language in 1830. He later became acquainted with German. He later became acquainted with Hebrew. He never had any real acquaintance with any academic understanding of Egyptian, even though Champollion's things have been published. He did not demonstrate any curiosity about that language, along the lines that Champollion was promoting. But, I believe that he was a translator in the way that he defined translation, which he also applied to his revelatory revision of the Bible. He never went back to the Latin texts, the Greek texts, the Hebrew texts that existed that he could have gone back to. He translated instead, the Bible, as he called it, as a revelatory act. And that's how he translated the Book of Mormon. He looked in the hat, he had the seer stone and he dictated the translation. And it was an act of revelation. It wasn't translation in the way that we define.

GT:	01:51:26	It sounds like you think it's kind of a combination of maybe a legitimate translation with some 19th century theology.

Michael:	01:51:32	Right. And that was how people defined translation. I quoted in my analysis of the Book of Mormon, what the American Encyclopedia at the time published in 1898, which was really based on the Encyclopedia Britannica. It defined translation, not as word for word, but as keeping the spirit of the original, keeping the general meaning of the original. That was the meaning of translation when Joseph Smith was a young man. And Brigham Young said that if the Book of Mormon were translated again, he said this publicly in the 1860s, it would be substantially different from what we have as the 1830 Book of Mormon. Well, how could that be, if it was word for word? How could it be substantially different? And Brigham Young said that God expects man and translators to act according to their knowledge. And Joseph Smith translated according to his cultural knowledge at the time.

GT: 01:52:38   Ok. Well, that's very interesting.

Women Have Had the Priesthood Since 1843!

Introduction

In 1992, Dr. Michael Quinn published an essay stating that women have held the priesthood since 1843. It was one of the reasons church leaders cited in excommunicating him. This will be an interesting contrast to our conversation with Dr. Jonathan Stapley, which did not endorse the idea that women held priesthood. Both Stapley agree that women don't hold priesthood office, but Quinn is bolder in his claims than Stapley. I asked Quinn what he thought about the Ordain Women movement. Check out our conversation....

GT: 01:52:55 So my last question is, I'm kind of going back to your introduction. You know, the church has really changed a lot in regard to openness. We've come out with the new Gospel Topics essays.[11] There's even one on women and priesthood. If you had published this book with Maxine Hanks[12] today, and by the way, Maxine has rejoined the LDS church, do you think it would be as controversial today as it was back in 1992?

Michael: 01:53:26 Well, in that one essay I did not advocate giving women priesthood ordinances of office, such as high priestess or deaconess or whatever. I just simply said that the evidence indicated that what Joseph Smith taught was more important than any office. The priesthood, the high priesthood,

---

[11] See https://www.lds.org/topics/essays?lang=eng

[12] The book is called "Women and Authority," and can be purchased as https://amzn.to/2OrEWAg

the authority of God he had given to women from 1843 onward. And that's how they understood it. Those who were his contemporaries in Nauvoo understood what they had received was priesthood. I'm not sure if that would still raise accusations of apostasy. It's a different world now. And the openness, I welcome. My attitude is better late than never. However, in the process since the rise of the Internet and the use of the Internet by evangelical Protestants to use Mormon history as a battering ram against the faith of Mormons, I think we've lost an entire generation before these essays of openness and transparency came out. And without that kind of openness, members of the church, whether they were ancestral Mormons or whether they were converts, had no resource that they knew of to counter what they were being hammered with by evangelicals. Had the church in 1998 after the Internet was building, and it was obvious what evangelicals were using it for. I mean, you typed in what was a search that you could do on the worldwide web as it was initially called, "Mormon," the first hit you'd get were by evangelicals attacking Mormonism and using Mormon history as the weapon.

Michael: <u>01:55:44</u>　Had those essays come out in the late '90s or even in the early 2000s, it would have been a resource that members of the church when they were hit by this needed and didn't have. So, although I do have the philosophy, better late than never, and I applaud these essays, Gospel Topics essays, I grieve that they didn't come out 15 years earlier.

GT: 01:56:10   So I want to make sure we're clear on your 1992
                         essay. You said women have had the priesthood
                         since 1843.

Michael: 01:56:22   But this did not involve office.

GT: 01:56:24   Ok, so what does it involve?

Michael: 01:56:25   Because the priesthood is greater than office and
                         offices were defined as appendages of the
                         priesthood. Priesthood is the authority to act in
                         the name of God, and women had that.

GT: 01:56:38   So, the authority to do what?

Michael: 01:56:41   To heal, which they did, to give sacred ordinances
                         to other women, which they continue to do in the
                         temples. And it was through the endowment that
                         women were given the priesthood.

GT: 01:56:54   So women receive the priesthood, meaning the
                         power to act in God's name through the
                         endowment.

Michael: 01:57:04   Right, and the President of the Church would be
                         the one to define how far they could use that
                         priesthood. He praised them for healing. And so,
                         they had his blessing and healing. He said, "I turn
                         the key to you," even before they'd received the
                         priesthood when he organized them as the
                         women's Relief Society.

GT: 01:57:04   Joseph Smith.

Michael: 01:57:28   Joseph Smith talked to them as queens and priestesses even before they received the endowment. So, where Joseph would have led the church and allow women to go after 1844 is anyone's guess. But I only wrote about what he said and what the women he said it to when they received the keys, as he said, he had given them in 1842 and when he gave them the endowment and the priesthood as they understood him to say in 1843. I just affirmed this is it. This is what they have, and this is why they've continued to talk about having priesthood.

GT: 01:58:07   But women today don't understand that when they get the endowment that they get priesthood.

Michael: 01:58:11   No they don't. And they should.

GT: 01:58:13   Do men get a special priesthood with the endowment?

Michael: 01:58:17   No, they have to be ordained separately.

GT: 01:58:22   {chuckles} So this endowment is different for men as it is for women?

Michael: 01:58:24   Yeah. I mean the view of I think many of even leaders today is that men are the weaker sex and that they need to be propped up more spiritually than women do.

GT: 01:58:37   Ok.

Michael: <u>01:58:38</u>   So men have to be ordained to the priesthood. Women receive priesthood when it's conferred on them in the endowment, and I think that men do too, but they've already received it. They've received it separately as young men as 12-year-olds to prepare them for the endowment. Women don't need that kind of preparation. They are already spiritually endowed.

GT: <u>01:59:04</u>   At least that is the stereotypical thinking.

Michael: <u>01:59:04</u>   That's the stereotypical view. And I'm willing to adopt that because it's convenient to help people understand this issue that women have a preparation that is separate for the endowment than men do.

GT: <u>01:59:19</u>   Ok, so what do you think about Kate Kelly's movement with Ordain Women?

Michael: <u>01:59:24</u>   I understand it. I don't support it.

GT: <u>01:59:24</u>   You don't support it?

Michael: <u>01:59:31</u>   No, I understand it and I don't think it's necessary for women to be ordained to an appendage.

GT: <u>01:59:31</u>   Why not?

Michael: <u>01:59:36</u>   Women don't need an appendage to have the priesthood.

GT: <u>01:59:38</u>   They've already got the priesthood.

Michael: <u>01:59:40</u>   They've got the priesthood.

GT: 01:59:41   But what about the idea, why couldn't a woman become a bishop? Lead a congregation?

Michael: 01:59:51   If those who preside over the appendages of these offices, which is what the president of the church does, he's the president of the high priesthood. He could change that.

GT: 02:00:04   Is this a policy or a doctrine?

Michael: 02:00:05   Well, that's a good question. And the women who are in Ordain Women argue it is a misogynist policy that stretches back to medieval Christianity. And I can't argue with that historical perspective. Misogynist Christianity won out over Gnostic Christianity. Gnostic Christianity allowed women to be priests and priestesses and idolized the divine in women. The Christianity that won out at the various councils of Nicaea and various others is a misogynistic Christianity which not only denied priesthood to the women but spoke of them as if they were a creature of Satan. And that was the theology of the Medieval Church, which has trickled down even to Protestants, except the most liberal of them, like the Quakers and also those who allow now the ordination of women. I don't revolt at the idea of the ordination of women, but I think the ordination of women in the Mormon context must come with the instructions, the blessing if need be, the ordination authorized by the President of the church who is the president of the high priesthood, which is what Joseph Smith said he was giving to women.

GT: 02:01:45   Would you welcome if women could begin to lay
                       hands on the sick, like they used to?

Michael: 02:01:51   They have no need to ask anyone's permission to
                       do that.

GT: 02:01:53   Really?

Michael: 02:01:54   No, in my view.

GT: 02:01:55   So they could do that now with the temple
                       endowment?

Michael: 02:02:00   Yes. And when Joseph F. Smith was president of
                       the church and he would travel to visit state
                       conferences and people would ask for blessings,
                       he sometimes asked Julina, his public wife of the
                       multiple wives he had, to perform the ordinances
                       of healing. And he would seal them, and she
                       would anoint.

GT: 02:02:00   Oh really?

Michael: 02:02:00   Yeah.

GT: 02:02:00   Oh I didn't know that.

Michael: 02:02:23   Yeah. And when they performed them together,
                       they both laid hands in the sealing ordinance of
                       the healing.

GT: 02:02:23   Wow.

Michael: 02:02:35   It's like if it's good enough for the president of the
                       church and sweet Julina as a priestess in her own

right, holding the priesthood, why isn't it right for somebody today?

GT: 02:02:47   So if a woman did that today, do you think she'd get in trouble?

Michael: 02:02:54   Oh yeah. But I think it's her right?

GT: 02:02:54   It is her right.

Michael: 02:02:57   In my view, but it's a right that has been smothered, not killed but smothered.

GT: 02:03:03   But you wouldn't support ordination to high priest or...

Michael: 02:03:08   No! Why does a woman have to be ordained to an appendage which is how the scriptures themselves refer to these offices? These are all appendages to the priesthood. The apostle is an appendage to the priesthood. Bishop, elder are all appendages to the priesthood. Women have received the priesthood and they have the authority to act in God. And if the president of the church said they could baptize with that, you know, that's wonderful. They don't need to be ordained. They have the high priesthood. Why should they need it? But the president of the Church would have to say, because he's president of the high priesthood, "You can do it."

GT: 02:03:53   Well, let me ask you this question because one of the big problems in Africa in the '60s, especially under President McKay, was the fact that only white men could lead a congregation. Now in

1978, that all changed. And so now we've got, you know, one of the biggest areas of growth is in Africa, but there is still a problem in the church, especially in the third world or developing countries or however you want to phrase it about more women are active. We don't have enough men. Wouldn't it behoove the church and especially in some of these congregations that are just, you know, 80 percent women, they don't have enough men, to have a woman be the branch president?

Michael: 02:04:31   Let me talk a little bit about the cultural imperialism of Mormonism. If, to have a religious ceremony, you have to have a pipe organ in sub-Sahara Africa, how soon do you think women are going to be given the right to their privileges in sub-Sahara Africa by the men in Salt Lake City who are prophets, seers, and revelators? If they can't see that a pipe organ is culturally defined as spiritual, whereas in Europe and America, the drum is culturally defined in Africa as being an instrument of spirituality. If they can't accept that and allow that, how are they ever going to allow women to have the prominence that women should have in the congregations of the church throughout the world? So, I see the cultural imperialism of the church requires that converts of the Church become not only American, not only Western European, but Utah in their attitudes.

Michael: 02:05:48   And this is a prison in my view for the growth of Mormonism to continue to link cultural attitudes of the west, of America, and of Utah, with being a good Mormon. And, I wish that they would acknowledge that that is a restraint that is not required by the commandments of God, not required by the revelations. And that men and women could dress according to their cultural beliefs and practices as they wish to in church meetings, which might be wonderful, bright colored dresses for the women and bare chest for the men. And why not? If this is a part of their culture, why should we impose the tie and white shirt on people who are devout and faithful? And why should we impose pipe organs on them if drums are their religious cultural symbol musically?

GT: 02:07:00 I mean, I do remember. I'm trying to remember which book it was. I read a book and I want to say it was in either Ghana or Kenya perhaps, but there was a woman in the '60s that was leading a congregation in black Africa.

Michael: 02:07:00 That was Nigeria.

GT: 02:07:15 Nigeria. Okay. Thank you. And she was essentially the bishop, but the church wasn't organized. So then 1978 comes. Well they made her the Relief Society president. But it does seem like, because I've heard people say, well, we can't allow women to hold the priesthood because in Africa that would be terrible. But it wasn't a problem in Nigeria.

Michael: 02:07:38 Yes, but in my view, that's an illusion.

GT: 02:07:39 That's an illusion.

Michael: 02:07:40   That women hold the priesthood once they are endowed in the temple. Now, to the degree that they're allowed to exercise it right now, they're only allowed to exercise it in conferring priesthood upon other women.

GT: 02:07:40   Right, in the temple.

Michael: 02:07:58   Within the temple, through those ordinances, but the wording of the ordinances, I don't need to go over, but that is the only legitimate exercise of their priesthood that the president of the high priesthood currently authorizes them. He could do more.

GT: 02:08:15   He could allow them to be a branch president in Africa.

Michael: 02:08:15   Yes.

GT: 02:08:19   I mean, wouldn't that even accelerate church growth more?

Michael: 02:08:23   I think so, but you would inevitably lose traditional members of the church just as the Reorganization which is now called the [Community] of Christ, lost almost half of its devout membership when the president of that church proclaimed a revelation, "Thus sayeth the Lord" that gave women the right to priesthood.

GT: 02:08:45   So that would cause a schism, you think?

Michael: 02:08:47   I think so. So, I was talking with Matt Harris. We'll wrap this up here. I know we need to do it, but one of the things that Matt Harris is doing, he's a scholar, do you know Matt by chance?

Michael: 02:08:47   Yes.

GT: 02:08:57   So he's been doing a lot of work with World War II to present and he gave some fascinating insights into President Kimball with the way that he was able to prevent a schism[13] because he felt like that could have happened with the race ban.

Michael: 02:08:57   It could have.

GT: 02:09:15   And President Kimball brought the apostles along, it took about four years, but he brought them along and I guess a prophet would have to do something similar to what President Kimball did in '78 to bring the quorum along to prevent a schism.

Michael: 02:09:31   Except I don't think it would take as long because there isn't the kind of indoctrination that the church has had about the inferiority of black Africans concerning women. There has been a dual message about women. Women can become goddesses, but they can't become bishops. How does that make sense? That doesn't make sense.

GT: 02:09:31   I agree.

Michael: 02:10:07   Because the messages have been mixed about women over time and even to the present, I think that it would be an easier thing to provide, first of

---

[13] See our interview at https://gospeltangents.com/2018/05/29/how-kimball-persuaded-apostles-to-agree-on-lifting-the-ban/

all, the knowledge to women that they already have the priesthood if they'd been endowed. And then if the president of the priesthood wants to allow them to have administrative roles in ministry, then you know, I think that the way could be more easily adjusted, and I don't think that would cause the schism in Mormonism that was potential with the giving of the priesthood to blacks. And there were people who left. And I'll give you an example of this. I can't remember now even who this was, but sometime late in 1978, I was talking with somebody who'd been on a business trip from Utah to the East Coast, that weekend.

Michael: 02:11:05   And so the announcement was made and on Saturday he was up in Boston and one of the stakes there, maybe the Boston Stake, was having stake meetings and he attended them on Saturday and he said everyone was celebrating, you know, this wonderful announcement and how wonderful it is we have a living prophet who can make this change that this is just warms our hearts. And then the next day he moved south because he had meetings in Columbia, South Carolina on Monday. And so, he checked into a hotel. He took an early flight to Columbia, South Carolina and decided on the system of having a morning and afternoon meetings to attend Columbia Ward that had an afternoon meeting. He went into the meeting and you know how Mormon meetings are. The chaos in the hallways trying to keep people quiet. And the church meeting space itself is always a problem.

Michael: 02:12:10   The organist has to lift up the volume to drown out all the talking. He went into the South Carolina Ward, Columbia, South Carolina. Absolute silence. People were walking like they were in a funeral in the halls. No one mentioned the announcement. The Bishop did not have to call for quiet. Everyone was quiet and somber before the sacrament meeting began. As he began his remarks, not a single reference to the announcement of revelation that Spencer W. Kimball gave.

GT: 02:12:10   Wow.

Michael: 02:12:52   And this was as witnessed by one guy going to church meetings in Boston, compared to Columbia, South Carolina. So yes, I'm sure there were devout members of the church in the deep South and South Carolina isn't even the deep south.

GT: 02:12:52   I served my mission in South Carolina, in Columbia.

Michael: 02:13:16   And although they certainly claim to be the southerners, but I'm sure there were devout members of the church who could not stomach that change.

GT: 02:13:26   I will say that there were not very many black people in most of the words I served. It was still tough back in the '80s.

Michael: 02:13:37   Yeah, and that was years after. So yeah, it's prejudice or tradition. Cultural traditions can

outweigh the power of a testimony, whether it's
in Jesus as a Christian or whether it's in Joseph
Smith and the Book of Mormon in addition to the
testimony of Christ. and sometimes that will
drive people away from another faith tradition
and go to a faith tradition where they're more
comfortable culturally.

GT: 02:14:14   All right, well Michael Quinn, I really appreciate
the time you spent here. And, once again, thank
you for participating at *Gospel Tangents*.

Michael: 02:14:14   Thanks for the opportunity.

Epilogue

GT: 02:14:27   I hope you enjoyed our conversation with Dr. Michael Quinn. Thanks Michael. I really appreciate it. It was a lot of fun.

GT: 02:14:33   If you'd like a transcript of this, please click the Yellow Subscribe Button at GospelTangents.Com and I'll send you this and all future transcripts. Also, if you'd like a paperback like we've got here, those are available at our website at Amazon.com.[14] Just do a search for Gospel Tangents. Please get all updates at our Facebook page at www.facebook.Com/GospelTangents. We're also on twitter @GospelTangents. You can also get transcripts individually at our website, GospelTangents.com/shop. Finally, make sure that you subscribe on Apple podcast page. Just do a quick search for a Gospel Tangents there and give us a five-star review while you're at it. Thanks again for listening. Your support helps create more Mormon history classes and podcasts such as this, and so I really appreciate you listening. Please share with your friends. Click here to subscribe, here for a transcript, and over here you'll see some more of our great videos. Thanks again.

I hope you check out our next guest, Steve Mayfield. He discusses Mormons and Crime. We'll be talking about good guys and bad guys, from John D. Lee and the Mountain Meadows Massacre to Mormon spies, to his early days in the FBI and the Patti Hearst kidnapping.

---

[14] See https://amzn.to/2P6WjY2

Steve: More importantly, I was there during a well-known case, this little kidnapping case you might have heard of, Patti Hearst. I wasn't an agent, but I was involved in that in the fact that I was assigned to the Berkeley office of the FBI where the kidnapping occurred, for about three or four months. Then I came back to San Francisco. I was there the day she was arrested and brought in.

Thank you so much for listening. Make sure that you like our page on Facebook.com/GospelTangents. You can subscribe for free at YouTube at YouTube.com/GospelTangents. We are also on Twitter @GospelTangents, as make sure that you subscribe on iTunes so you don't miss any of our episodes. We hope you'll use this as a valuable resource to learn more about Mormon history!

Additional Resources:

MacKay & Hamer – Community of Christ Perspective

John Hamer was ordained to the First Quorum of Seventy in October 2017. Lachlan MacKay is an apostle for the Community of Christ

120: Start of RLDS Church & Mormon Schisms Tour
https://gospeltangents.com/2018/01/26/start-rlds-church-related-schisms-tour/

119: Surprising Word of Wisdom Insights from an Apostle
https://gospeltangents.com/2018/01/24/surprising-word-wisdom-insights-apostle/

118: Mormon Followers of the Prophet James Strang
https://gospeltangents.com/2018/01/21/mormon-followers-prophet-james-strang/

117: Alice Cooper's Roots in Lively Mormon Schisms
https://gospeltangents.com/2018/01/16/alice-coopers-roots-lively-mormon-schisms/

116: Different Succession Claims: Other Mormon Groups
https://gospeltangents.com/2018/01/13/different-succession-claims-mormon-groups/

115: Strange Kirtland Temple Ownership Problems
https://gospeltangents.com/2018/01/10/strange-ownership-problems-kirtland-temple/

114: Comparing LDS & RLDS Temple Worship
https://gospeltangents.com/2018/01/07/comparing-lds-rlds-temple-worship/

Jonathan Stapley – The Power of Godliness

Dr. Jonathan Stapley Discusses evolution of LDS Priesthood Ordinances

Anne Wilde on Modern Polygamy

Anne Wilde, founder of Principle Voices, modern-day Polygamy expert

096: Ervil Lebaron: Polygamist, Assassin
https://gospeltangents.com/2017/11/16/ervil-lebaron-polygamist-assassin/

095: FLDS-Centennial Park Rivalry
https://gospeltangents.com/2017/11/14/flds-centennial-park-rivalry/

091: 3rd Manifesto Causes Schism: Apostolic United Brethren
https://gospeltangents.com/2017/10/31/third-manifesto-causes-schism-apostolic-united-brethren/

Interview with Remnant LDS Church

Jim Vun Cannon, Counselor in the First Presidency of the Remnant Church of Jesus Christ of Latter Day Saints

067: What are Remnant Church Views on Temple Worship?
https://gospeltangents.com/2017/08/20/what-are-remnant-beliefs-about-temples/

066: Women Will Not Hold Priesthood!
https://gospeltangents.com/2017/08/11/women-will-never-get-priesthood/

065: Joseph was a Monogamist!
https://gospeltangents.com/2017/08/17/joseph-was-a-monogamist/

064: What's the Order of Enoch? Consecration in Modern World
https://gospeltangents.com/2017/08/14/order-enoch-reinterpreting-consecration-todays-world/

063: Jim Tackles DNA & Book of Mormon
https://gospeltangents.com/2017/08/08/jim-tackles-dna-book-mormon/

062: 18 Revelations to Gather to Missouri! Remnant Church Scriptures
https://gospeltangents.com/2017/08/05/18-revelations-gather-missouri/

061: What's the RLDS Perspective on Succession Crisis?
https://gospeltangents.com/2017/08/02/whats-rlds-perspective-succession-crisis/

060: From Convert to First Presidency in 5 years!
https://gospeltangents.com/2017/07/30/convert-first-presidency-5-years/

059: Found! A Literal Descendant of Aaron!
https://gospeltangents.com/2017/07/27/found-literal-descendant-aaron/

Click here to subscribe (on iTunes), click here for a transcript. (You can also get one at Amazon.com), and over here you'll see some other videos that we've done on Youtube.) We hope you'll use this as a valuable resource to learn more about Mormon history!

Be sure to check out our blog as well at https://GospelTangents.com to find information about future guests and projects we are working on. We would also like to partner with artists and musicians to produce a documentary on this and other topics. Please email us at GospelTangents@gmail.com if you're interested.

Thank you for your generous support!